The Best Pet for Me

Is a CAT
a Good Pet for Me?

Theresa Emminizer

PowerKiDS
press™

New York

Published in 2020 by The Rosen Publishing Group, Inc.
29 East 21st Street, New York, NY 10010

First Edition

Editor: Elizabeth Krajnik
Book Design: Rachel Rising

Library of Congress Cataloging-in-Publication Data

Names: Emminizer, Theresa, author.
Title: Is a cat a good pet for me? / Theresa Emminizer.
Description: New York : PowerKids Press, [2020] | Series: The best pet for me
 | Includes index.
Identifiers: LCCN 2018048092| ISBN 9781725300965 (paperback) | ISBN
 9781725300989 (library bound) | ISBN 9781725300972 (6 pack)
Subjects: LCSH: Cats–Juvenile literature. | Pets–Juvenile literature.
Classification: LCC SF445.7 .E48 2020 | DDC 636.8–dc23
LC record available at https://lccn.loc.gov/2018048092

Manufactured in the United States of America

CPSIA Compliance Information: Batch #CSPK19. For Further Information contact Rosen Publishing, New York, New York at 1-800-237-9932.

Contents

Crazy About Cats

Have you ever seen a furry cat **basking** in the sun? Or watched a fuzzy **feline** playfully **swatting** at a feather on a string? Maybe you've heard a kitty's sweet meow as it asks for food or its rumbling purr as it rubs against your ankles. If so, you've probably wondered— could a cat be the right pet for me?

Cats are some of the world's most popular pets, with good reason! These cute creatures are full of fun. However, before getting a cat, it's important to consider what it takes to be a cat owner. Read on to find out!

Pet Report

Did you know that cats are good for your health? Studies show that cat owners have a lower risk of heart disease than people who don't own cats. Cat owners are also less likely to suffer from **depression**.

Cats make great reading buddies. They love to sit on top of your book!

A Brief History of Cats

Scientists think that people began **domesticating** cats around 12,000 years ago. Cats are skilled hunters of mice and other pests that make their homes in stores of foods such as grains. People realized that having cats around meant fewer pests, and the cats were well fed.

Even though many cats today enjoy comfortable lives, they haven't lost their hunting **instincts**. Wild cats teach their kittens to hunt by bringing them dead animals. In the same way, pet cats often bring their owners "gifts" in the form of dead animals such as birds. If this happens, don't be alarmed. It's natural and a sign of love!

Pet Report

Cats are carnivores, which means they only eat meat. They need food that's high in animal protein. You can feed them dry or wet cat food or cooked or raw fresh meat.

In ancient Egypt, cats were highly respected, so much so that killing a cat was a crime. **Archaeologists** have uncovered many cat mummies, such as the one pictured here.

Feline Fast Facts

Cats are very interesting creatures! They have great night vision. They're able to see in the dark six times better than a human can. Cats can also hear sounds that are too low and too high for humans to hear. Their ears have 32 **muscles**, while ours only have 12. This makes it possible for them to move their ears to find where a sound is coming from.

Cat whiskers are sensory detectors, which means cats use their whiskers to learn about their surroundings. They also use their whiskers to judge the size of openings.

Pet Report

If a cat has ever licked you, you know that their tongues are rough. That's because a cat's tongue is covered in tiny, backward-facing hooks. These help cats pull food to the back of their throat.

Did you know that most cats are left-pawed?

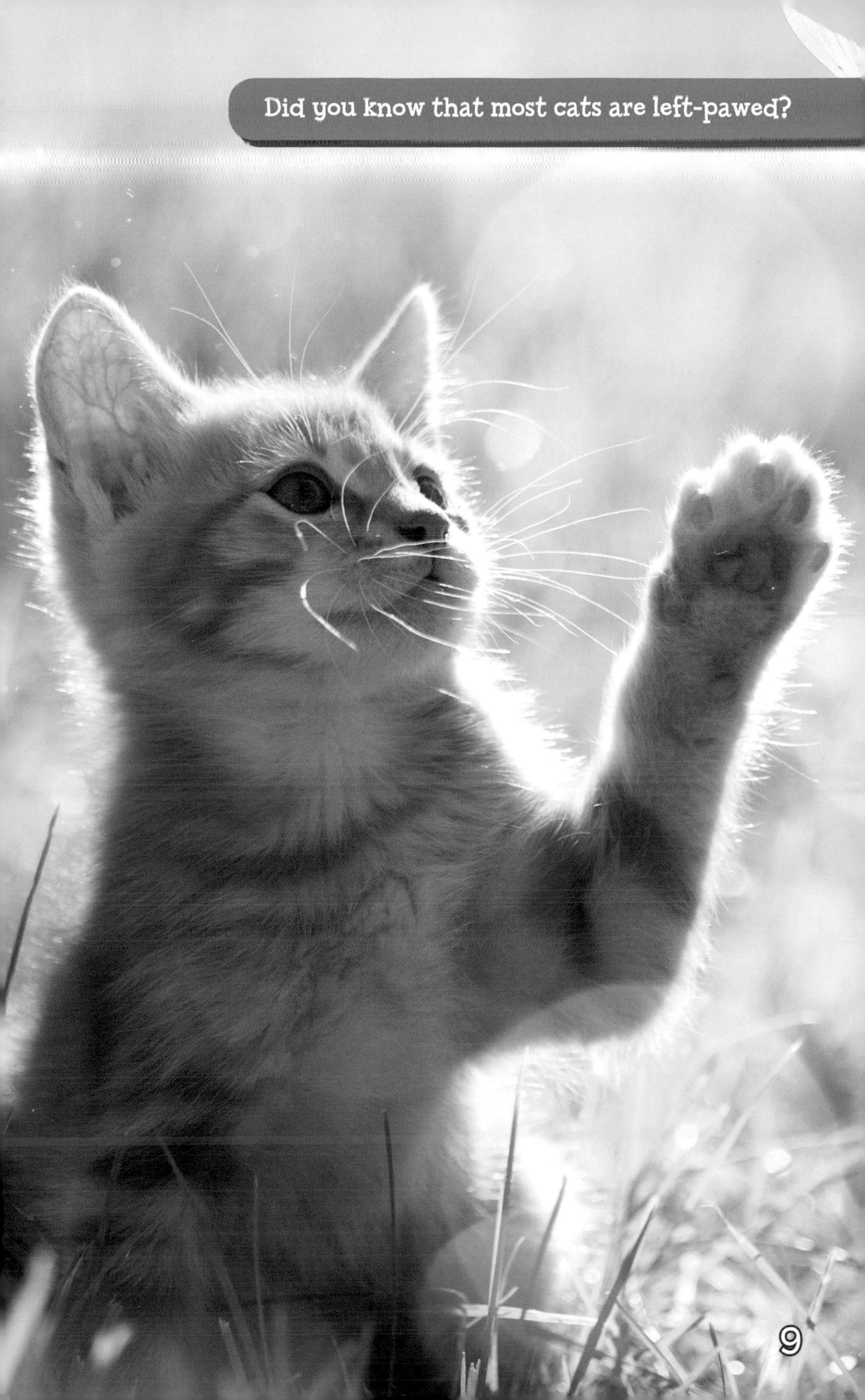

From Kittens to Cats

Cats are usually born in litters of three to five kittens. Newborn kittens only weigh about three or four ounces (85 to 113.4 g). They're blind for the first week or so and open their eyes when they're about seven to ten days old. Kittens begin walking when they're about two weeks old. They're able to leave their mothers when they reach eight to ten weeks old.

Cats reach adulthood around one year of age. They can live to be about 20 years old. Before getting a cat, it's important to make sure you'll be able to care for it for the rest of its life.

Pet Report

Most cats nap during the day and are active at night or very early in the morning. Playing with your cat in the evening and feeding it its largest meal before bed will help your cat sleep through the night.

In 1970, a Siamese cat in Oxfordshire, United Kingdom, had a litter of 19 kittens. This is the world's largest litter of domestic kittens on record.

Kinds of Cats

Before you get a cat, it's important to decide which breed, or kind, is right for you. The first question to ask yourself is: How much **shedding** are you willing to deal with? Long-haired cat breeds shed more than short-haired cat breeds. Long-haired cats need to be **groomed** more often.

Next, how large would you like your cat to be? Maine coons can weigh more than 20 pounds (9.1 kg)! However, Singapura cats only weigh four to eight pounds (1.8 to 3.6 kg). What breed of cat do you think will suit your home?

Pet Report

It's important to **spay** or **neuter** your cat. Depending on where you buy or adopt your cat from, the cost of spaying or neutering may be included in the price. If not, it's important to schedule an operation with the vet.

If you adopt your cat from a rescue shelter, such as the ASPCA, it will most likely be a mixed breed. Mixed breed cats are commonly called domestic shorthair cats.

Behavior and Training

If you get a kitten, the first thing you'll need to do is train it to use a litter box. For safety, very young kittens should only be allowed in one room rather than allowed to roam the whole house. Choose a spot for the litter box that's easy for your kitten to find. Most cats prefer to have their litter box in a corner. Make sure to clean your cat's litter box at least once a day.

To train your cat effectively, it's important to use positive reinforcement. This means rewarding your cat with treats, **catnip**, and petting when it **behaves** well.

Pet Report

Make your house a safe space! Some houseplants can be poisonous to cats, and they can choke on strings and other small objects. Kitty-proof your house before bringing your new pet home.

You can train your cat to come when you call it, shake hands, walk on a leash, and even use the toilet!

Reading Body Language

It's important to understand how your cat is feeling. Its body language will give you clues.

Cats rub their heads on things to leave their scent behind, to say hello, or to show affection. Slow blinking is another sign of love. To cats, closing eyes in your presence is a great sign of trust. If your cat **kneads** you, that means it feels safe and happy.

When a cat is content, its tail will stand straight up or sway slowly. When it feels stressed, or worried, its tail will hang down. If your cat's tail is puffed up, it may feel threatened, or scared that it will be harmed.

scratching post

Pet Report

Cats are naturally curious, but they can become bored easily. To keep your cat happy, be sure to play with it often and offer it safe toys that hold its interest.

When a cat is frightened, it will arch its back and puff out its fur to appear larger. This is the classic "Halloween cat" pose.

Meowing, Yowling, and Purring

Cats can be noisy! If your cat is meowing, it's probably trying to tell you something. Most often, cats meow to say hello, to get your attention, to ask for food, and to ask to be let in or out. However, constant meowing can be a sign of distress, or unhappiness or pain. You should take your cat to the vet if you think something's wrong. Female cats yowl when they're in heat, or looking for a **mate**. They growl and hiss when they feel threatened.

Many people know cats purr when they're happy. But did you know that purring also helps with bone growth, pain relief, and wound healing?

Listen carefully to your cat. What's it trying to tell you?

19

Caring for Your Cat

Adopting a cat will change your life! Cats make wonderful, loving companions. Before you decide to get a cat, make sure you've thought about all that's required to care for one. Are you ready to patiently and gently train your cat? Can you afford to take it to the vet and keep it healthy? Are you willing to clean up after your cat and buy food and litter whenever it needs it?

If you and your family can answer "yes" to all these questions, then you're ready to become a cat owner! You can adopt a cat from a shelter or buy one from a breeder. Which cat will you choose as your new best friend?

Many cats become another member of the family.

What You'll Need

Fee:	$0 to more than $3,000 for certain purebreds
Litter Box:	$2 to $40
Litter:	$20 for a 40-pound box
Cat Food:	$34 for a 12-pound bag of high-protein, grain-free dry food
Food Bowls:	$7 for a basic bowl, up to $140 for an automatic feeder
Cat Carrier:	$18 to $175
Vet Bills:	$50 to $300
Vaccines:	$45 to $85
Flea Control:	$50 to $150
Toys:	$10 to $75

Total estimated cost for beginning supplies:
$236 to $4,019

Glossary

archaeologist: Someone who studies the tools and other objects left behind by ancient people.

bask: To lie or relax in pleasantly warm surroundings, especially in sunlight.

behave: To act in a particular way.

catnip: A type of mint that has a strong smell that is attractive to cats.

depression: A state of feeling sad.

domesticate: To breed and raise an animal for use by people.

feline: Cat, or related to cats.

groom: To clean and care for an animal.

instinct: A way of behaving, thinking, or feeling that is not learned.

knead: To press and squeeze with hands or paws.

mate: One of two animals that come together to produce babies.

muscle: A part of the body that produces motion.

neuter: To remove the sex organs from a male animal.

shed: To lose or cast aside something, such as hair, as part of a natural process.

spay: To remove the sex organs of a female animal.

swat: To hit someone or something with a quick motion.

Index

Websites

Due to the changing nature of Internet links, PowerKids Press has
developed an online list of websites related to the subject of this book.
This site is updated regularly. Please use this link to access the list:
www.powerkidslinks.com/bpfm/cat